The Most Important Book in Human History

By

Michael Phillips

By Michael Phillips

The Seven Laws of Money
Random House and Shambhala Classic (with Salli Rasberry)

Honest Business
Random House and Shambhala Classic (with Salli Rasberry)

Simple Living Investments
Clear Glass Press (with Catherine Campbell)

Marketing Without Advertising
Nolo Press (with Salli Rasberry)

Gods of Commerce
Clear Glass Press

Commerce
Clear Glass Press

Table of Contents

Appendix

Pro commerce. Why not?

(PHOTO: RUSSIAN MILITARY TRANSPORT)

The *modern world* in the first quarter of the 21st century is defined by a kitchen with drinkable hot and cold running water, refrigeration, cooking facilities with gas or electricity, a sanitary sewage line, a wide variety of globally sourced inexpensive food and connection to the global communications network.

Most educated people are not aware that modern life is 100% the construct of modern commerce originating only two centuries ago in the 1800s with the industrial revolution.

Many people see modernity as the byproduct of *science, technology, economic growth, medicine* and/or *government*. Some think that *religion* or *capital* may have caused it. Those are not the driving force for modernity. Simple examples can disprove all of the above false gods. To understand modernity's source, readers must understand both the history of modern commerce and the nature of modern commerce.

Let us take the simple counterexamples first.

- *Science* and *technology* are seen by many as the source of the modern world. The photo above, of a Russian military transport, shows that for 75 years the USSR was just as competent in science and technology as any part of the contemporary world. But anyone who went to the USSR in those 75 years, as I did in 1981, knows that it wasn't part of the contemporary *commercial* world. Ordinary people, and, often even the most elite people, lacked clean drinking water, clean water for bathing, heated living conditions, good transportation outside of the two major cities, and adequate food, including vegetables and meats. People in the USSR, despite their advanced science and technology, did not have department stores or grocery stores, much less the ability to travel around their own country or start a business.

  Today Cuba, Venezuela, and North Korea have most modern science and technology available to the elite members of their society, but not to 95% of the people. High tech weapons are fully operational from tanks to automobiles, x-ray machines, lasers, radar, and computers. Technology exists in nearly fully operational form, but nothing there resembles modern commercial life.

- *Economic growth* and *capital.* Two of the richest per capita countries in the world are Saudi Arabia and Brunei. No one who has visited these countries would doubt that they have used sophisticated building technologies and transportation to appear to be modern commercial nations. They have GDP and capital, but they lack even one shop that can manufacture a modern bicycle, a pack of cigarettes, or a pencil.

- *Medicine.* Medicine and associated sanitation ideas are found fully developed in Johannesburg, Kabul, and New Delhi, but they have a surrounding population with average lifespans of 54 years, 47 years, and 60 years. Modernity does not come from medicine and sanitation, but the two together have brought us out-of-control population growth in much of Africa and India.

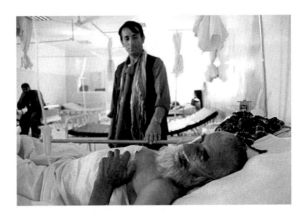

- Lastly, does *religion* bring the modern world with it? Max Weber suggested that Protestantism's ideas were the source of the modern world. That doesn't explain the very modern bootstrap nations of Japan, Taiwan, and Singapore. Japan has a religious base of Shinto and Buddhism; Taiwan is Daoist, Confucian, and Buddhist, while Singapore is equal parts Hindu, Confucian, and Christian. They are all modern but without Protestantism.

- Is *government* the source of the modern world? Of course we find stable and modern government everywhere from Communist East Germany to North Korea, but rarely did it or does it generate our modern world.

No, the modern world is not explained by any of the standard ideas, not even close. The preceding stark and dramatic list of examples shows how each of the standard ideas about our modern world's source is wrong. *Science, technology, economic growth, medicine, government, religion or capital do not create modernity.* Much more is needed to understand why the modern world is **solely the by-product** of *modern commerce.*

Modern commerce is the engine of modernity. The other elements are train cars (technology, medicine, etc) pulled by the engine of modern commerce.

'Modern commerce' is not a single entity

What are we talking about when we talk about 'modern commerce'?

We can go to a national capital like Bamako in Mali and see many shops, a movie theater, a fancy modern hotel, and a few bed and breakfasts, yet it doesn't feel like a modern commercial city. Why not?

To answer that question we first need to examine what business categories there are. I find three categories of business and two other related forms. I explain the first three here: http://phillips.blogs.com/goc/2012/01/original-ideas-10.html. Bamako only has the first two.

One form of commerce is **'trade.'** Trade was the first and is the most enduring form of business. The guy who sells cigarettes to prisoners in a prison is in trade. A thousand years ago the native Illini traders who took

Lake Michigan shells to the Mississippian tribe to exchange for pottery were in the trade category of business. A product or service is exchanged for money or a monetary equivalent. The trader has a markup on the goods and services that allows him to buy or make replacements and have enough surplus to remain in the business. A local farmer's market, a flower shop, or a local ice creamery is in trade. Each needs just enough markup to buy more inventory and stay in business.

The second category is **'clientry.'** The object of clientry is to sell a good or service that generates a lifetime relationship with the client. A clientric form of business would be a dentist, doctor, lawyer, designer, Japanese tea ceremony teacher, banker, or investment counselor. A few teachers, such as Socrates and Pythagoras, ran ancient clientric businesses. The goal of a clientric business is a lifetime relationship.

The most recent category of business is **'industry.'** We don't find industry in Bamako. While some ancient furniture makers used mass production techniques, the great innovations in industry came around 1800 when water power and steam power were added to the process. The goal of industry is to reduce the market price of the goods or services. These reductions in costs are usually achieved by economies of scale, including expanding the market, as well as by applying technology. Any chain business is in the category of *industry* whether it is the local insurance broker, the coffee shop, the Home Depot, the Nissan outlet, or Delta Airlines.

The presence of industry, particularly the head office of some industry, is a sign of modern commerce.

The other two forms related to business are 'non-profits' and government-owned businesses. Non-profits are nothing but a 'business' that, at least ostensibly, has a non-business social objective and applying to it a tax definition. They don't have an owner and their net surplus must be plowed back into the business. Non-profits can be trade, as in a local children's clothing resale shop. They can be clientric, such as the church-run kindergarten that provides services for all the family members as they age. Or they can be industrial, such as the Red Cross with offices everywhere.

Then there are government businesses such as the Army PX, which is a department store the Army runs, or the US Postal Service, which is a semi-government owned shipping and delivery service. These are weird entities: They can be internally subsidized. They can be efficient or inefficient. They just aren't really businesses. They are pseudo or imitation businesses because they don't have to make a profit.

Being able to recognize the variety of business categories is a first step in recognizing the elements of modern commerce. Understanding the varieties of commerce requires an act of imagination.

If all business looks the same, then the nature of modern commerce is hard to discern. Understanding that trade is aimed at making each sale work, that clientry is aimed at a lifelong relationship, and that industry is aimed at reducing costs helps to see what business is really about and that industry is new and novel. Reducing costs has created our modern world.

The first paragraph mentions Bamako, the capital of Mali. Bamako doesn't feel like a modern commercial city because nothing is manufactured there or created there and it has no company headquarters, as would be expected in a modern commercial center.

Values of modern commerce: meritocracy

The first chapter gave examples establishing that all the reasons people use to explain what created the modern world are wrong.

The only source of the modern world is modern commerce, beginning with the industrial revolution.

The three main varieties of modern commerce are trade, clientry, and industry. Understanding these three categories is necessary to see the elements of business around us. Not knowing these categories obscures the nature of modern commerce.

Standing in front of a local flower shop (trade) with its owner-manager or standing in front of your dentist's office (clientric) is very different from sitting in a Segafredo coffee shop just like tens of thousands of people in twenty countries around the planet (industry). (Segafredo, for those who know only Starbucks, is a multi-billion dollar business headquartered in Villorba, Italy.)

Only the unique presence of 'industrial business,' the category that aims to reduce costs with economies of scale defines the modern commercial world.

This chapter is one of four. Three concern **the values that promote modern commerce** and allow it to thrive. Meritocracy, diversity and openness are the three values and each gets a chapter of its own in this sequence.

The final chapter covers the history of modern commerce which I hope will offer a solid basis for understanding the sources of modernity. History explains how the 'industrial' model evolved out of meritocracy, diversity, and openness as these qualities entered society to coalesce into modern commerce.

You can't see the role of meritocracy, diversity, and openness as vital values of commerce merely by walking through a shopping mall. Nor can you see it by working for a profit-making business. If you could, everyone would be a pro commerce advocate. I only saw these three values while working as a consultant, all over the world, with more than two thousand businesses and two thousand financial statements.

What is meritocracy? And why does it matter so much to modern commerce? According to the *Merriam-Webster* dictionary, the word 'meritocracy' was first used in 1958. I believe that. It is a recent term and a recent concept. It is also a vital concept if one is to understand the power and importance of modern commerce.

A meritocratic society is one that values individual merit over all else. The two most common forms of society that are **not meritocratic are hereditary class societies and tribal societies.**

In an hereditary class society all important functions are offered to fellow members of the hereditary class, usually in birth order. In most of the world with an hereditary class society, such as England, France, Turkey, Spain, Brazil, the Philippines, and hundreds more, valuable places in society go to the oldest son of a member of the elite class. That would be the top management position in the company, the legislative seat held by the father, the partnership in the watch business or any other valuable position. Sometimes the entire family receives the benefits of the hereditary family membership for entrance to the college, clubs, and familial occupations.

The other form of society that is not meritocratic is a tribal society. In a tribal society all the benefits of the tribe accrue to other members of the particular tribe. A tribal society can also have an hereditary family structure and often does. All of Arabia, Africa, and South America are tribal societies. In Jordan, the person chosen for a job or apprenticeships is always a member of the same tribe. In Jordan, for example, these tribes are: Abbas, Malik, Mustafa, Quraysh, Ghassan, etc. Tribes have very extensive cousin relationships so all jobs go to 'cousins'.

In China the tribes have names such as Wang, Li, Zhang, Liu, Chen, Xu, etc . A nice apartment might become available in Shanghai, but only a member of the Liu network will hear about it.

Some tribal societies use a little bit of merit in assigning valuable social assets. At a trucking firm run by the Malik family, the cousin who is best with numbers might get the accounting job in the firm's office. In the Kahn family dance school, the top teacher might occasionally be the best dancer. But, the head of the school will always be a Kahn.

In the very few meritocratic societies, such as the U.S. or Israel, we have the rarest of strange behaviors. When we have a position to fill, say a nurse at a VA hospital or a line cook in a French restaurant, we actually interview many people for the job and ask everyone we know to send us the most competent referrals. Then we pick the one who will fit into the business and do the best job. That is meritocracy. It is unheard of in most of the world and is largely irrelevant outside of modern industrial commerce.

Because merit is relevant to high levels of production, management, and technology it becomes obvious that meritocracy is a keystone of industrial commerce in a modern commercial society.

Values of modern commerce: diversity

One of the values that make the modern commercial world possible is 'diversity.'

Unfortunately, many who might otherwise love modern commerce have the wrong idea about 'diversity' as it applies to commerce. Diversity in this context does not mean gender difference, melanin difference, or difference in income level, religion or ethnicity.

(PHOTO: TOP DEVELOPERS AT BELL LABS.)

A group of five people who are on the board of a Sacramento seed supply company could include an elderly rich lesbian, two black academics, one of whom is gay, a Taiwanese mother of two, and a Filipino male nurse and they still might have no diversity of worldviews. They could all be Marxist or all hardline anti-sugar foodies. Their diversity of gender, melanin, or ethnicity is not the kind of diversity that 'diversity' in modern commerce is about.

Real diversity is about different worldviews and different life experiences. A former Navy fighter pilot, a Buddhist monk, an aeronautic engineer, a young graphic designer and a Public Relations expert from Washington DC, even if they are all white males, could be a much more diverse group than the members of that seed supply company. Their talent and experiential diversity may be just what's needed for a modern commercial management team.

What is wanted in a modern commercial society is 'diversity' of experiences and worldviews in order to get real vitality in decision-making about technology, marketing and management.

Real commercial-grade diversity generates creativity and originality. It is absolutely necessary for meritocracy. That is why all modern commerce evolved first in big coastal cities where genuine diversity has always existed: Amsterdam, London, New York, and Glasgow.

In the early 1970s I was asked by a planning agency in Japan what made the U.S. such a technical prodigy. My answer was in a small phone directory I carried with me, the 1960 New Jersey Bell Lab internal directory. I showed them a few pages of names. This is the laboratory that invented the transistor, found the background radiation of the universe, and had 6 winners of the Nobel prize in physics. The names I showed were: Narain Gehani, William Shockley, John Bardeen, Arno Penzias, Steven Chu,

Horst Stormer, Daniel Tsui, George Smith, Robert Wilson, Herbert Ives, Joseph Mauborgne, Russell Ohi, Mary Torrey, and George Stibitz. This list didn't look like an ordinary American telephone directory. These people were brought from all around the world to create a team of the top global minds. It was true diversity of the modern commercial sort.

You won't find a list of names like that in Mexico, South Korea, France, or Poland. You won't find the kind of genuine commercial diversity like that in most of the world.

That is the kind of diversity that allows a modern commercial company to be innovative in technology, marketing and management.

Modern commerce needs openness.

A synonym for openness is honesty. I have always preferred to talk in terms of openness because 'honesty' is the absence of deceit. Openness is an institutional condition of trust where deceit can not even take root. A small difference, but I prefer the open environment to one that depends on constantly evaluating whether 'honest' people are being honest all the time.

Why would modern commerce need and promote openness?

The true underlying require-ment for modern commerce is trust. Openness is the way to create trust over a broad array of circumstances. Commerce is carried out over vast distances and between untrusting people.

The original form of trade appears to have been one tribe putting its goods on a river bank and another tribe putting its goods on the opposite river bank. No trust was needed. The buyers on each side of the river were allowed to return to their side when the trade was considered acceptable by both sides.

Currency was a way to make trade easier by exchanging a universal coin, gold, for the goods and services. Little trust was needed. Stories about drug gangs selling merchandise for money then keeping both the drugs and the money are common fare in the world of fiction. Mostly fiction. For most transactions, currency works fine in lieu of trust, but more complex transactions such as shipping require more.

This is why some tribes with strong internal trust were able to carry on trade over long distances for several millennia. Phoenicians, Jews, Chinese families, and the West African Fulani tribe became long-distance intermediaries. A tribal member was present at each end of the transaction to verify the transaction. There was openness in the tribe or family.

More complex transactions over time required legal documents and courts. Both these elements required openness. The lawyers had to follow open published legal standards and the court records had to be public as well. The same became true of insurance contracts, stock exchanges and entire legal systems. All of these institutions required openness to be the basis for trust in commercial transactions.

The early days of modern commerce were built on all these open institutions, bond markets, stock markets, legal systems, contracts, and trade treaties. As corporations emerged in commerce in the 1850s, laws and public filings became the form of openness. Today, openness in securities filings and banking transactions is vital for the survival and expansion of modern commerce.

It is hard for us to remember that every commercial institution plays a role in keeping the level of trust high for modern commerce. Banks guarantee the safety of their checks, credit cards, and bank accounts. So do we when we give credit cards and checks to restaurants and retailers. These businesses are trusted for their confidentiality about our cards. They are subject to openness at some level of audit, government examination, and reputation.

The most important role of openness is inside of businesses. Almost no one can run a business if they can't trust other people in the business, and they expect openness about all management relations. If a manager gives directions to a peer or subordinate who fails to carry out the directions or report back accurately, then that peer or subordinate is forced out of the business as are other people who fail to report the breach. New people are not hired in the first place if an aura of deceptive behavior hangs over them. There is politics in management and some people are trusted more than others. Some are more loyal than others.

Openness is a core value that is generated in modern commercial markets and is necessary inside modern commercial business.

I am the person who made international currency possible with the development of multi-bank issued credit cards that allow modern people to travel the world, and buy and sell goods and services. That whole credit card system is based on the long history of interbank trust which in turn is built on interbank openness. For the first few decades of bank credit cards, they all used an 'Interbank' symbol.

Trust is the core value of modern commerce that allows a tribeswoman in the back woods of Cameroon to sell her goods in Charleston, South Carolina. Trust is based on a vast series of institutions that rely on openness.

Pro commerce history

There were many elements that went into the first successful trading nation. Holland in the 1600s was the first major global trading nation. Trading posts had been developed on sea lanes by the Phoenicians, the Vikings, the Chinese, the Viennese and, specifically in the North Sea region, by the Frisians (the main source of the English language). Bookkeeping, a vital element, came from Milan. In the 1600s, Holland, focused on Amsterdam, was the source of government bonds markets, international shipping insurance, the stock market and other open bidding markets and, importantly, salaried tax collectors (source of trustworthy tax collection). The Dutch were a unique people on the planet. They had created a representative democracy with many elected offices. The Dutch Republic united the Netherlands with seven provinces in 1581.

The Dutch were noted by all visitors in the 1600s as the most egalitarian people on the planet. They were also the most tolerant. They had absorbed the Jewish exiles of the Spanish Inquisition of Spain and Portugal. Amsterdam in the 1600s was the center of technology, the center of the Enlightenment, and the center of publishing in all of Europe. (See Jonathan I Israel's *The Dutch Republic*.)

The Dutch military conquered England in 1688 and transferred all the major Dutch financial institutions to England where the Dutch Head of State, William of Orange and his wife, became the King and Queen of England, William III and Mary. With the English Parliament that welcomed them, they created the Bill of Rights of 1689 — the major source of modern English law and the model for the American Bill of Rights.

Holland was prosperous in the 1600s, as was its settlement in the American colonies, New Amsterdam (later New York). New York became the source of most American financial institutions and, with the creation of the United States and the American Constitution, it became a central financial force. New York's representative, Alexander Hamilton, played a major role in building modern financial ideas into the structure of the 13 united colonies.

Using the Dutch financial tools, England, with a much larger population, became the largest global trading nation from 1700 until 1945.

In the history of commerce these towering international commonwealths, England and Holland, generated an entire future generation of entrepreneurs and giant trading businesses. The Dutch and British colonies were gigantic new markets and training stations for homeland officials. The colonies created entrepots where the second and third sons of the hereditary elites, who were denied any serious role in their own countries, could find important positions of power. That was the beginning of meritocracy.

The colonial cities also provided great 'diversity' in the commercial meaning of that term. Colonial networks were the origins of modern commerce. Colonies created markets for Dutch, British and other local goods and the navies to transport them.

England is considered the original home of the Industrial Revolution, as water power and steam power were introduced to accelerate wool, cotton, and ceramic production lines. The revolution spread to the rapidly expanding United States in the 1850s with the expansion of the West which allowed the meritocratic offspring of the colonial states' hereditary elites to open the vast new reaches of America along with the commercial entrepots created by the soaring number of immigrants from the entire world.

Three other ingredients played a role in this historic development of industry.

The original Freemason Grand Lodge was founded in London about

1720 and spread around the world by the end of the 1700s. Freemasonry became the home of diverse men who could trust each other. (In some sense it is a pseudo-tribe.) It therefore provided the backbone of trust and finance for the industrial revolution and its expansion in the 1800s provided finance for the American frontier. There were thousands of Masonic Lodges in the U.S. and Europe in the mid 1800s. As late as 1920 there were over 3 million freemasons in the U.S. Good literary sources are Seven Bullock and Joel Mokyr.

The second was the application of the new technologies of animal husbandry and horticulture to farming in the mid-to-late 1700s in England and Holland which increased production dramatically, creating free labor to supply the emerging industrial revolution factories. Good source is Joyce Appleby.

Third, and last, was the widespread publication of Adam Smith's _Wealth of Nations_ which helped leaders and thinkers understand the nature of the explosion of industrial production and trade that surrounded them.

In retrospect, the industrial revolution was the convergence of many small but critical elements, along with the three major elements I have identified. Meritocracy had to emerge from within societies ruled by hereditary elites. The Dutch and British colonial systems made this possible. In America, the vast Western expansion made this possible even more so.

The diversity necessary for commercial creativity and technological innovation was also a byproduct of this international mingling of people and cultures in the many urban cities of the colonies.

Lastly, the emergence of safe spaces for open and tolerant men of diverse backgrounds and the institutions of modern commerce that they fostered was essential. Democracy and law were vital, as were the Freemasons and similar institutions that the Dutch, English, and Americans promoted.

Evolution of business

The modern world is the byproduct of modern commerce, not of science, technology, medicine, economic growth, government, capital or religion. Instead, the usual list of things driving commerce is merely a list of commerce's byproducts. I have shown that modern commerce is made up of three distinct types of business: trade, clientry, and industry. Only industry has created and been an integral part of modernity.

The distinct attributes of modernity and the sources of vigor for modern commerce are meritocracy, diversity, and openness. These developed in nations with institutions of law and finance that made trust pervasively available with their structural openness (courts and banks). That modernity, in turn, was able to thrive in the world of aggressive colonial trade and the expansion of the American West where the meritocratic sons of fortune could escape their hereditary elite families. Lastly, the mixture of institutions that favored openness among strangers (e.g., Freemasonry) which promoted meritocratic values and generated life in truly diverse urban communities were the fertilizer for the thriving of modern commerce.

All of this is new to most people. It is also fairly obvious to most people when they reflect on it.

There is a less visible reason that modern commerce is a stunningly successful human creation which has brought us such extraordinary benefits in such a short time (two hundred years). That reason is that modern commerce is driven by evolution.

Evolution is composed of two elements: steady random change in the existing conditions and selection for the desirable changes. That is a perfect description of modern commerce. Business is constantly in flux and constantly rewarding businesses in the direction that favors individual needs, tastes, and desires.

Everything in modern commerce evolves. The 1,000 square foot local food outlet in 1860 with barrels of goods and a proprietor has evolved into vast chains of supermarkets with hundreds of thousands of square feet each, tens of thousands of packaged goods, and hundreds of thousands of employees. The airplane has evolved from a one-person kite using a one cylinder gasoline engine with wing and tail controls to a 400-person behemoth that flies thousands of miles at hundreds of miles per hour in all weather as part of a global corporation transporting millions of strangers every month.

Businesses evolve. They are born in the flux of market changes, sometimes infinitely small like a river changing its course. They grow when they appeal to customers and they die when they become part of a bigger consumer driven corporation or they shut their door. In the United States at the beginning of the 21st Century there were over half a million new businesses* started and only one-third of them survived ten years. Evolution gives new life to the world of commerce and continually improves the lives of its beneficiaries.

Commerce in the modern world thrives on evolution and creates a wonderful variety of products, services and livelihoods. Just as evolution creates a nearly infinite variety of species in the natural world from which we all enjoy the benefits and some distresses, it does the same in the modern commercial world.

*https://www.bls.gov/bdm/entrepreneurship/entrepreneurship.htm

Appendix

Appendices deals with questions from lectures and discussions.

Poverty

'Poverty' is often used as an accusation against the world of modern commerce by people who are anti-commerce.

'Poverty' is a term without solid definition. A group is labelled living in 'poverty' in Central Africa where starvation is rampant, clean water doesn't exist, and shelter is seasonal. A group is labelled living in poverty in the United States when most of its members have autos, television sets, and smart phones.

I draw a distinction between what modern commerce, as a voluntary system, can do and what it can't do.

Poverty does exist in the world of modern commerce. Poverty also exists in most of the world outside of modern commerce. It is common in most of Africa. Poverty existed nearly everywhere on the planet for thousands of years before modern commerce. Famines were common and frequent.

Because modern commerce is so astoundingly successful in creating riches and abundance, it is subject to special criticism because it often carries poverty with it. A complaint of irony.

The reality is that poverty is unrelated to modern commerce. As unrelated as bicycles and fish.

Poverty is a subset of income distribution; poverty is an issue of governance. If there were a reason to redistribute income, it would be the responsibility of government and/or governance. That is what communism and other forms of tyranny are all about.

An example of the separation of modern commerce and government is Singapore, which is a city-state with over 5 million citizens. No poverty exists in Singapore. It is not allowed. Singapore is a modern commercial city-state. Singapore is also a benign socialist tyranny. It has a vast public housing infrastructure, a very effective police system, and many charitable organizations. It doesn't allow poverty.

It is always possible for **government** to support a person with little education, no skills, a few children, and no desire to work. Modern commerce doesn't have that facility; it is a system of voluntary relationships. But most businesses could not afford to hire that person.

Modern commerce creates opportunities for one person or group of people to sell to another person or group of people. One group of a million people acting together can produce a product (a thumbdrive) and sell it to a billion other people. The whole transaction is voluntary on a massive scale.

Poverty is a consequence of government neglect or omission, or the absence of government. Poverty is separate from modern commerce. Government has the power to coerce; modern commerce is a voluntary system.

Positive sum

We owe a debt to John von Neumann, Oskar Morgenstern, and John Nash who developed, in the 1940s and 1950s, the mathematical foundations of game theory. Nash was the subject of the movie 'A Beautiful Mind' about a mathematician who ended up in a psychiatric institution.

Game theory introduces the concept of 'positive sum.' Understanding modern commerce is difficult without the concept of positive sum. Games can be positive sum, zero, and negative sum. Chess and checkers, like nearly all games, are zero sum. One person wins and the other person losses.

Positive sum is where the outcome of the game or activity results in the total of the losses and gains being greater than zero.

Most people see the world as zero sum. Popular political ideology argues that rich people get rich at the expense of poor people. In most tribal and historical narratives one tribe or nation gains in land or population while the neighbor loses land or resources. That is zero sum.

Modern commerce is a positive sum world. People become rich by appealing to the tastes and desires of many other people who are better off when they buy the goods or services offered by the person who consequently becomes rich. A positive sum. The people who bought the goods or services were better off and the people who didn't were generally not made worse off.

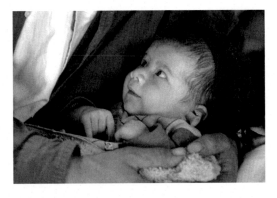

There are other positive sum parts of the modern world. Medicine is an example. Getting the polio vaccines made everyone who got the vaccine better off because they didn't get polio like earlier generations. Even the people nearby who didn't get the polio vaccine were better off because there was less polio in the community to be communicated.

Much of surgery, sanitation and other aspects of modern medicine are positive sum activities.

Much of technology is positive sum. That is usually true of a bridge that makes life easier for people who live on both sides. That is true for ambulances that seem to save many lives. It is also true for life vests.

The idea of positive sum arrived recently. Fortunately it is a way to accurately understand that modern commerce is a voluntary human activity that has a net benefit for most people that doesn't come at the expense of others.

"Red in tooth and claw"

This familiar phrase comes from Tennyson's *Memoriam:* (ode 56) which is about Jesus and the mountainous desert landscape around him:

> "'Who trusted God was love indeed
> And love Creation's final law
> Tho' Nature, red in tooth and claw
> With ravine, shriek'd against his creed"

We moderns often love to spend time in nature to escape the *rat race* of modern life. We find nature to be so peaceful and magnificent. Biologists suggest we don't see the less visible aspects of nature. Those lovely song birds are eating smaller organisms as they fly and light on tree branches; the smaller organisms are eating spores and other microscopic organisms. The trees are generating hundreds of poisons as are the mushrooms, to keep their hostile plant parasites and predators away. Indeed, most of nature is 'red in tooth and claw'.

It is modern commerce that is unnatural and thrives on cooperation.

It is in a modern commercial office where an Orthodox Israeli Jew works enthusiastically supervising a project consisting of a team of a Jordanian Muslim engineer, a Kurdish accountant from Turkey and a Brazilian Roman Catholic graphic designer. They all lunch regularly at an Indian-Punjabi restaurant. Occasionally they are joined by their Mormon and African Baptist higher ups. That is not unusual in a modern commercial office. Nobody is even conscious of the historical wars that their ancestors have fought for thousands of years.

Modern commerce is where diverse people get along. Unlike Jakarta or Kuala Lumpur where locals openly kill third-generation Chinese in the streets.

In the rarest of human activities, modern commerce, 99% of all daily activities are cooperative. The thirty suppliers to Cliff's Hardware store are all helpful and make suggestions for better display and better lighting. The lawyers, accountants and maintenance people are all as helpful in promoting the business as they can be. They are generous and kind every day.

Of course there are disputes and antagonism. Which is why modern commercial societies have vast legal structures to resolve commercial disputes — often using mediation and arbitration with unbiased outsiders. Still, the practice of law is a vast enterprise designed to maintain stability and comity wherever possible.

On the whole, nearly all businesses thrive on the cooperation and goodwill of their suppliers, advisors, employees and patrons. All these relationships are voluntary and nearly all are convivial. Even inspectors and law enforcement in modern commercial societies try friendship and courtesy as their first tools of behavior.

In general, modern commerce is overwhelmingly cooperative. A wonderful attribute that is not often visible.

This environment of comity should not be mistaken for a commercial world of 'morality'. Morality concerns good and bad. Commerce is like Darwinian evolution. It is an amoral world. In the modern world of commerce good people can do poorly and bad people can be successful.

Modern commerce thrives on meritocracy, diversity and openness and creates an environment of comity but it does so in an amoral system. Modern commerce is evolutionary and exists independent of moral systems. It delivers goods and services to individuals based on their needs, desires and tastes not on their individual moral standing or moral claims. It is effective and efficient in its amoral evolutionary nature.

Modern commerce, in the form of many ships and corporations delivered oil to Israel for many decades when the oil producing Arab nations were boycotting Israel and trying to destroy it.

The end

Extraordinary efforts went into the review and editing of this book. Special thanks for very careful and detailed work by:

Cynthia Phillips
David Boxenhorn
Scott Phillips
Andrea Widburg

With additional help from Sonie Richardson, Laura Phillips, Hans Deuel and Ann MacArthur.

Michael 1938 Phillips

Lives in San Francisco where he began a career as a banker, founding the marketing research department at the Bank of America.

He was the organizer of the first multi-bank credit card (MasterCard) that led to the first international currency.

As president of the Point Foundation, created with funds from *The Last Whole Earth Catalog*, he funded the corporate social responsibility movement and many environmental projects. He championed open business and was the first person to promote random selection of legislators.

He has spent 45 years as a business consultant, founding the Briarpatch Network, the first small business network, which spread to Sweden and other parts of the world. He has written eleven books including the most well known, *The Seven Laws of Money* published by Random House and co-authored with Salli Rasberry, and *Marketing Without Advertising* from Nolo Press also co-authored with Salli Rasberry.

Made in the USA
San Bernardino, CA
26 August 2017